at Home with Disquiet

Erin Wilson

POEMS

CIRCLING RIVERS
RICHMOND, VIRGINIA

Copyright © 2019 by Erin Wilson

All rights reserved. No part of this book may be reproduced in any form, including electronic, without permission in writing from the author.

CIRCLING RIVERS
PO Box 8291
Richmond, VA 23226

www.CirclingRivers.com

ISBN: 978-1-939530-10-3 | paper
Library of Congress Control Number: 2019955656

ISBN 978-1-939530-14-1 (hardcover)
Library of Congress Control Number: 2020938881

Cover photos by Erin Wilson

Visit CirclingRivers.com to subscribe to news of our authors and books, including book giveaways. We never share or sell our list.

dedication

With gratitude, for those who made me,
my parents, Ownie, Zella and Aurele,
my children, Ana and Liam,
and James, my husband

Contents

dedication

    Tracks Disappearing over a Field | 13

i.) **chyak-chyak**
    wherein Jackdaw introduces herself

    Jackdaw Chyak-Chyak | 17
    Fingernails of Grain, Which Kept Safe My Childhood
      (after Aleš Šteger) | 18
    Freckled | 20
    Portrait | 21
    First Fort | 22
    Cantilevered | 24
    Taking the Big Canoe to Childhood | 25
    Names Listed on the Inside Cover of a Family Bible | 26
    Some Day You'll Know My Name | 28

ii.) **giaaaa**
    wherein Jackdaw begs her mate for food

    A Small Room with a Generous View | 33
    From Dayton, May 2000 | 34
    Five | 35
    Pulling Carrots, Cabbage, Turnips, Late Fall | 38
    Because of Light | 39
    Hands Remember Best | 40
    Lines from Movies (A Letter to Van Gogh) | 41
        i. Before the Gunshot | 41
        ii. Spit from the Top of the Stairs | 42
        iii. Recognized in Passing | 42
        iv. Glint, Gleam, Glom and Glimmer | 44
    From the Garden | 45

iii.) **kaaaarr**
    wherein Jackdaw perceives threat

    Considering Their Pale Faces | 49
    A Mother and Her Two Children, A Holy Trinity of:
      How do you pronounce your vowels? | 50
    The Black Draft | 51

He Is Fishing (Suite) | 52
    Music | 52
    It Was This Big | 54
    An Untitled Rothko | 55
Seed | 57
What's Good for You | 58
It's Late | 60

iv.) **kya-kya-kya**
wherein jackdaw experiences distress and excitement

One Shade Away from Never Having Been | 63
Tangerine | 65
Sex with You is a Strange Violin | 66
Statistics, 2012 | 67
Genealogy, Hope and a Christmas Turkey | 68
A Winter's Night, A Love Poem | 70
Anthem | 71
Three Teens Sleep in a Tent | 73
A Rural Mom Warns Her Daughter about
   Dangers in the City | 75
The Roan | 76
Birdsong | 77
The Mother | 78

v.)
wherein Jackdaw can be trained to imitate human speech

Children of the Imperceptible | 81
Body of Complaint | 82
Mare | 83
Real Things; Not Junk—
   Swimming in the Aux Sables River | 84
The Shine on the Road's Blacktop When It Rains | 86
Cancer (Suite) | 88
   Healthcare | 88
   Radiance | 89
   To Live | 92
   Human Chain | 92
Homecoming | 94
Gentrification | 96
Jacquard | 98
Nature and Nurture | 100

Decibel | 101
Regarding the Fullness of Emptiness and Silence | 102

vi.) wherein Jackdaw reconciles
with the world

Centripetal Force and a Lull in the Stratosphere | 105
It Seeks Cracks and Enters | 107
Rarity Keeps the Raven at Bay | 108
Meditation Beside an Unkempt Lot | 110
Grappling with Gratitude | 111
Atlas of Anatomy for an Artist | 113
Rust | 115
Citrus and Sugar | 116
Culmination and Collapse | 117
Almost | 118

vii.)

Agrarian Landscape with Fan Brush | 123

Acknowledgments | 126
    Previously published in… | 126
    Quotes | 127

Tracks Disappearing over a Field

Late day bruise of clouds—
    does the sun love the world and show it most in its leaving?

Stippled fringe of conifer and a crosshatch of white birch,
    breath freezing the collar into a stiffened mast.

It is a painted glass plate you walk toward that holds the ache like art,
    cows sheltering from cold in a copse of divested trees.

Queen Anne's lace, its lesser known sister-self
    (who warms to its skeletal presence?)—empty palm thrust
    upright.

A bus delivers a child home, late, maybe the last run of the day,
    to a dog's bark dying down in the distance.

A crow passes overhead and caws three times,
    a signatory to existence, removed, inviolable.

You carry inside an opening of possible hunger that sharpens
    as you move, a hot dinner heating the edge of this cold landscape.

Fox tracks leave the road, enter the field, then disappear.
    What does this warm red drum amble after?
        What could there possibly be?

i.) **chyak-chyak**
wherein Jackdaw introduces
herself

Jackdaw Chyak-Chyak

I wanted to be alive
like a human being
from out of history,
a man with a coat alert on a chaise,
or a woman stayed by a bodice,
and so I stuck myself with corvid feathers.

I wanted to pound to pound to pound on heaven

and so I fucked some books
against a wall
and stuck my fingers
inside myself *(kaaaarr)*.
I wanted to sing sweetly
like an angel
or a mom
and so I chirred quietly
to my little ones *(giaaaa)*
through the soft waft
of steam that rose
from a well-cooked pot roast.

I wanted to believe
my skin would stay.

I wanted to hear God say
(in lines, not tongues or heavenly gestures)
words that would remain.
I wanted hell to vanish.
To not exist. As it doesn't.

Except here. Except sometimes.

Fingernails of Grain, Which Kept Safe My Childhood
   (after Aleš Šteger)

— for my father

There is no learning ahead of me. All of the learning to happen is behind me.

You gave the silk of your manness like a white flag. You surrendered. Oh, you gave yourself willingly, nightly, like the moon to the sky.

There were nights beyond the barn—but only in theory.

All else rested nearby, illuminated by your sphere.

We were swollen ticks, glamored in the thickness of our bedclothes. The rooster quivered once, but it was only a settling of its feathers. The nervous hens closed their eyes and dropped all that was held by their bodies into their laps. Dappled slates, they awaited their fates, while the voracious weasel burrowed meticulously. Everything was in its place, from the forehead to the furred paws.

The engendering:

1. Nest inside your body with now's narration: now come here, now shovel shit, now pound some nails. A saga, for instance, is a carrot pulled from the ground when you're hungry.

2. Hold things: axes, buckets, springs and greasy metal workings, knives, forks, mom, me, the thread fed through the eyes for jigging.

3. Be—and never worry.

The wheat is poor. Or the wheat is rich. The wheat is enough if parceled stoically.

Everything is to be gained.

All will be lost.

Freckled

My face tasted of sweat
and my hair smelled like
a dirty suitcase.

    What did I know?

I was on a new shore,
inserting my fingernails,
using every scrap of strength
I could scrape from my
just-now-growing,
just-now-unfolding
finger muscles,
forcing the clams
to give up their shape.

    I had no idea. Death?

No. I practiced against the tear
of the hale gird of elastic.

Then chucked each clam,
a broken wallet, into
a pile. They clattered.
Piled. Clattered.
And then slipped

from one another.

Portrait

I see these things but never wonder how I am made.
For example, Howard, across the street, drunk and disheveled,

weaving, then disappearing behind his window row of colored bottles.
My grandmother's fat arms full of lunky brown paper bags

bricked with his groceries, crossing the street. On the bottom of her
    TV stand,
in the brass wire tray, a scrapbook. In the scrapbook, hundreds of
    newspaper clippings

hoarding the residue of hundreds of black keys each, two particular
    oddments.
One, ominously Psalm 23, the thunderous words,

the authoritative sculpting of the calligraphic script.
Two, the article about the Tehkummah streaker.

Like font at our feet, the stubborn iron pedal on her Singer sewing
    machine.
Her morbidly purple toe. Her rose powder puff comporting its round
    container.

The summer powder coated me. Her sweaty pound of lye.
Her cut red hands. All the inevitable sweating and stinging.

First Fort

Behind the punch-clock, out back of the hotel, in the woods,
while adults are sewn to sheets, to registers, to highways—

we are a better version of adults.

Our eyes are hot and our bodies connected.

If their eyes were concise enough to trespass our shirts,
to behold our soft new breasts surging,
an egg would clog their throats,
a thrombus block their breathing.

We're twelve and our minds,
our minds are so green they oscillate.

We make a room in a clearing.

Or rather the space between six large trees presents itself
and invites us into a secret chamber in ourselves.

We stand in place and moult.

Clearly our minds are treetops.
How easy to make an oven.
Beds are no work at all.
With a little pressure
a precise cleanliness
implies our floor.

Our superior cunning adapts garbage
to surfeit the parameters of what's needed,
a garland of dead leaves weaves a window,

a branch ripens to a broom,
the wind and wavering shadows
pleat the workings of a wide-wending clock.

When we turn the knob (the knot on a tree)
our whole minds work.

We unearth wine bottles with our fingertips
and delicately touch their sacred collars—
then handle them roughly—
various green hues eye-dazzling with electrical sparks,
vacillating flutes accruing to paramouring densities
at their bulbous bottoms.

Our hearts rhapsodize and lift.
Our underarms sting with the gravity of mushroom scent.

To see, we force our blood flowers downward,
like red birds back into a black box,
and harness their beating.

Freckled pure pleasure, our faces fret our work.

Form. From out of air we generate form.
Our fort exclusive, personal,
the center of a world we'll build upon,
until we get bored
and it's buried.

Cantilevered

Our house was never Pentecost bright,
but a more lukewarm #23, whitewash.
Vinyl siding outside, sensible.
Inside: curtains, cushions, neat and narrow.
My mother smoked and read romance, bored.
Regularly vacuumed vagrant ash.
We ate from white plates: gray meat,
root vegetables and gravy.
The TV came on again at six p.m.
having been turned off briefly at five o'clock.
The only talk of god was, well, none.
But I prayed in private, read the Bible
(where on earth did it come from?)
in my parent's alcove window,
Twelve years old, eyes cast upward.
A small prickly pear sustained itself
on a living room end table
in a terracotta pot.
Flowered sometimes.
I stole behind locked doors in socked feet
coaxing mosquitoes onto my body,
high-breathed, impassioned,
anxious for penetration.

Taking the Big Canoe to Childhood

Chi-Cheemaun means "big canoe" in Anishinaabe

The first time I returned
to the country of my childhood,
each farm, each swamp,
each cedar hedge and each split-rail fence,
towered so tall I felt them,
these things on the outside,
looming like skyscrapers in my chest,
each familiar site an overpowering welt
of memory, on my tongue a braille dialect.

When I returned again,
Ward's Store shortened.

And again,
the swings behind my school
that used to breach the clouds
would only rend the feathered tops of fir trees.

Then again,
until the waves of the Great Lake
got pummeled and pounded almost still,
and the Chi-Cheemaun shrunk and sank
contiguous with the horizon.

Now I can go back or not—
it's all a plain I carry in my blood's swill,
a tableau that flows,

and yet might be broken like dry ice
with only the slightest mortal tapping.

Names Listed on the Inside Cover of a Family Bible

It was because we were hungry
we opened our mouths at daybreak
to take in the sky and whatever bird
crossed in front of us, kestrel, dove, robin.

It was because we were starved
we wandered over the hilltops and through the
stables and shops of one another, Corey, Tom,
me, David, Dwayne, Andrew.

We were famished and nothing real
could feed us, fish, radish, sorrow.

Nothing real existed in the same shape
as our emptiness, square, peg, pupil.

We met men, women, strangers, and took
them inside and felt, *we know you—a little*.

And then the children flocked out from us, Adam, Eve,
John, Edna, Théodule, Bertha, Leowen, Zella,
taking our blood chutes and increasing our hollows.

They left to wander over their hilltops,
deep-set eyes, already malnourished.

We shouted to the constantly fleeting shadows,
"Come back, Karrie, Michael, Timothy, Erin, Ana, Liam.
Reform us as we were. So we can know again our first aches.

So we can remember the precision of our first incomplete forms."

Then came years of hauntings and echoes,
a few rare hopes, and plenty of time, time—

Some Day You'll Know My Name

Let them not seek to discover who I was
from all that I have done and said....
Only from my most imperceptible deeds
and my most covert writings—
from these alone will they understand me...
— Constantine P. Cavafy

I came upon it by accident,
an abandoned farmstead
on a road that appealed to me
by name alone, *Blue Road,*
and so I turned down it.
I parked on the shoulder
and some cows ventured forth
from over a hill
toward the fence,
as though in greeting.
I opened the gate
and the great steer in the rear
stepped back
and nodded
and so I proceeded toward
the central empty structure.
Eons passed through
the barren apple trees,
the gnarliness of their limbs
declaring something true to me
that caused me the purest shiver.
I looked in through the open door
over the crumbled stairs.
White porcelain shards reposed
like entombed moths

and empty metal hooks
retained their form
curdled out from the wall boards.
I pulled back and stared away
from the collapsing cornerstone,
off into now pitted pasture.
In amongst the dried and steaming cow patties,
a small gentian, fire blue, struggled forth.

ii.) **giaaaa**
wherein Jackdaw begs her mate
for food

A Small Room with a Generous View

I've always dreamed of living a small life,
always wanted to be beloved of salt and pepper,
wanted to live directly above my pelvic girdle,
living to appreciate the allure of doorknobs,
the sex appeal of pianos.

I've always dreamed of living a small life,
maybe have a friend, maybe lose a lover,
maybe find a dog, maybe help a stranger.
Flowers are nice.

The only way not to live a small life
is by pretending one is lofty, living larger,
higher than, by untouching treetops,
believing that one is far beyond the hold of light and shadows,
by being executive of uberdom, a serf to no one.

I've always dreamed of living a small life,
accessing the extraordinarily fundamental,
taking the portal directly into being (which ends way past sorrow),
being the willing slave to marvel.

From Dayton, May 2000

— for Ana

Bread blossoms as metaphysical design.

And little printed sentences in books
lay planks right back to the beginning of our time.

Who wouldn't be enraptured by the riddle of your spontaneous skin,
the spark and empty lurching that make up your mind?

My mother's eyes rain down over your every crevasse and skein.
You kick and cry both above and beneath me.

Where once you beat inside of me,
oh, you still beat in me, still beat in me.

Nothing of the world will again be supine.
    And worlds be built with ladders.

Five

— for Liam

I.

Delightfully, after you tug upon the curled white string
waiting for the prize to be set free from the hilltop
(that you perceive as a mountain),
leaf litter up to your knees,
you hold the tampon out before you
as though you might hypnotize me.
You are five pretending to be seventy,
"Now, just who might drink tea up here?"

Little misunderstood things like this are darling.
You are darling, whose cup runneth over with Oolong.

II.

Only dark things move through the dark night, reproducing,
boosting one another, darkening darklings,
dark on top of dark. You hear the floorboards being
herded to the barn's stall out back. You hear dark
animals shuttling. Black milk shunts in ribbons
to be sucked up by dark creatures for sustenance.
You see hooves.

When a head tips back in ecstasy,
you're hurt by a blood-bed housing long white chompers.

III.

Even though it is a cross between a community center
and a living room (albeit lacking a couch)

you are initially shaken with fear.
That is, until you walk up the aisle
and lay your hands upon the casket.
With your face tipped forward
death's gleam shines up from the *it* and upon you
as though lighting your chin from a buttercup.

How relieved you are, "It's not grandma, only plastic!"

You rise onto your tippy-toes so that you might touch
the marbled chartreuse bowl that once held her.

    IV.

You *like* to be scared.
Not really.
Well, you like to be scared on a schedule.

For hide and seek you stand in a closet,
tell me not to be afraid
and then jump out.
You like to hide me in the laundry basket
then wonder where I am.

One time I am upstairs in your bedroom.
You run downstairs to get an apple
and then when you come back I am standing,
plain sight, but in a new location.

You cry and cry.
There are no words to console you.

V.

We lie on the couch, heart to heart.
You plump, then use my breasts for pillows.
Your weight begins to labor my breathing.
The soles of your feet graze my ankles.

"I'll always lie like this, Mommy."
"Yes," I chime, "we will always, always lie like this."

Pulling Carrots, Cabbage, Turnips, Late Fall

How hard must a mother be,
how tough, how enduring,
that the world asks her
to be the soft place,
knowing
she's only the soil
from which
food is plucked.

Because of Light

8:17 am and the sun's been cut,
    is angled from its rise,
projected off the black back of our neighbor's crest,
slant light through the front window of our small,
defunct, never-quite-clean wasp-like nest,
as if our walls were in fact made from pulp and spit.

I'm standing center room, disheveled,
same drab wool sweater I wear every day of winter,
    back lit,
my son at his desk,
too-much-time-for-a-child-away-from-play pallor,
chair squeaking.

"Whoa," he says, "the light like that—
you look just like Jesus Christ."

"Whoa," I think, divine surprise,
metaphorical equations pulling light
across his wan facial guise,
"And you sound just like him."

Our dishrag curtains glow,
seem to open like a veil,
    scrim.

Hands Remember Best

Beneath lamps, from
arm caps to stumps
to casters, weighted into the decks of
eight-way hand-tied spring coils,
the girls have slubbed their
voluptuous flubber into
every contour of
living room furniture, making
right full use of
the room's namesake,
and buried their
Rubens forms beneath
a cavalcade of
Klimt-colored quilts.
And while they make their
cherub puckers and
Cupid snores, I
snap a few candid pictures.
Later, boy do I get it!
"Not while I'm sleeping!"
she castigates,
but when she's awake
she'll not pose.
"Why do you have to take
pictures anyway?"
she neighs, stomps, then
coyly whimpers.
So I say, "Because daughter,
just like your little
sumac-colored coat
in our keepsake box,
memory lives most vividly
in a red velvet pocket."

Lines from Movies (A Letter to Van Gogh)

1. Before the Gunshot

Vincent, I'm not sure,
but I think if we listen hard enough
in our lives, something pure speaks.

Do we hear light?
Certainly it has volume.

Twice in my life something spoke.

It chose to enter the world
through my children's mouths.
Children are points of entry,
as you must have observed
with Maria Wilhelmina and Willem.

Can their phosphorescence forebear?

Each in his own measure, I suppose.
What happened to your lover Sien's brood?
Deep beneath the earth, I'm guessing,
where potatoes grow,
where you are now less defined
than sticks and bones,
and where I will go.

We'll break through the soil again, my friend,
and translate the radiance, translate it to fruition.

Now, that's the joke. There's no such thing.

As *fruition,* that is.

II. Spit from the Top of the Stairs

I'll tell you the first line, spoken by our first born.

It is Christmas—the season of lights.
Really, the season of trying to survive the darkness.
Ana is maybe six years old. Heh, the devil's number.
She has definitely been *not good*.
And so we do what all desperate parents do,
we threaten her with Santa.
She still does what she does. And we do what we do—
still buying the gifts, trying to compensate
for the something lost
with the cavalcade of shine and packaging.

On Christmas morning, as she peeks downstairs
from the top newel, she knows mathematically just how
bad she's been. Yet the tree shines
and the gifts are plenty.

With utter relief she sends upward this exclamation,
"Oh, more than enough!"

For effect
(like the repetition in your sous-bois series),
she repeats, "More than enough!"

III. Recognized in Passing

February 2012.
And as happens in Februaries
it has become dark very early.
We live in a small northern town

with only the basics,
a few neighbors, a peck of stores,
a bushel of mostly sold-off churches.
It's nearly 6 p.m. as my son and I
wind through the cold streets.

Cold, no opportunity here for overstatement.
Dark, but sometimes with the dalliance on snow
of moonshine.

We pass by the hardware store. We pass it.

And as we pass it the shop attendant,
ready to go home, turns off the lights.

Turns them off.

And Liam, at nine years old,
through the breadth of our ordinary
little lives,
notices this and notes it,
reports it to us, the world,
where our eyes should persist,
where our listening should linger.

It eases out of him like his breath
and gets caught and coated,
can be seen in the cold air
as witness to transitions—
"What an opportunity!"

What an opportunity, just this.
Always, just this.

IV. GLINT, GLEAM, GLOM AND GLIMMER

You tried, didn't you, Vincent.
F309a, "Trees and Undergrowth."

At times it was more than enough.
At times it was pure opportunity.

I have been reading Tranströmer lately.
You wouldn't have the chance to know him.
A certain poem stays with me and flickers
as I behold this painting by you, *of* you, it seems.
The Swedish words in repetition, *tänds och slocknar,*
tänds och slocknar (lights and fades out, lights and fades out).
(You see why I include the Swedish.) *Firescribbles,* made by fireflies.
After all we are all, through experiences, just trying to survive.

You are a gleaner, aren't you? Your purse filled at times
with hopeful glints and gleams, glommings and glimmers.

Even as your vital life bled away through the fields of golden braids,
your blood in that certain light...

As I sit before your painting, Vincent,

a great many things stream and wave across my face.

From the Garden

If it is unsayable (and it is unsayable) then how might my mother tell me she knows?
And if it can't be tamed by words or wrangled, how might I gauge my children's knowledge?

At the top of the stairs forty years ago my mother gently laid, like bottoms to bassinets, tomato
after tomato into boxed rows, trusting skin to balance carefully a weight that would seem to grow,
then covered the pale green abaci with newsprint.

If my mother does not know—then I will never understand anything.
A merciful grieving lives in my core and smells like a chord plucked between rotting and sweetness.

It was my child's mind which took all this in decades ago, organized it, and waited.
I planted a garden with my own children. Now we wait to see what grows.

iii.) **kaaaarr**
wherein Jackdaw perceives
threat

Considering Their Pale Faces

Fact: The manageable size of the baby paradise rose, with pinkish-lavender 1 - 1 1/2" blooms, offers a small garden big potential.

Experiential: We planted a few along the border of the garden we created with the edge of a shovel outside the kitchen window, when we bought the family home.

Fact: Even miniature roses are susceptible to what plagues their larger cousins.

Experiential: While you children toddled about, slipping happily in leaf rot, then swung on the tire swing, or later, hammered in the tree fort, I leaned toward the tiny leaves and scraped fat rose slugs into a tin can, or sometimes brazenly squashed them with a thumb nail.

Fact: For years the paradise rose struggled. Eventually, I left your father.

A Mother and Her Two Children, A Holy Trinity of:
   How do you pronounce your vowels?

> *When the quality is exceedingly high, it exceeds the limit of the form.*
> — Arvo Pärt

Standing in the Dollar Store with my Canadian children
after visiting their father in Ohio,
elated in the candy aisle,
practicing our pronunciation:
How do you say caramel? Carmul? CarAmel?
Me too! Me too!
And mum? Mom?
Mom, mom, mom... No,
MUm. I say mUm. I say mUm.
Caramel. Mum. Caramel. Mum.

In the car we stuff our faces full of candies.
All over the dark nights of Indiana the corn has become irrelevant,
the corn and the desolation, or
the tepid mornings and the winds to come.
In the car we travel raucously, laughing,
picking candy from our teeth,
missing deer.

The Black Draft

— in memoriam Grammy, age 66

At Birch Lake
the black painted turtles
have hauled themselves again
from the primordial muck;
they use their foreclaws
to hoist their shelled selves
onto trees
that fell to shore
fifteen years ago.

It's weird, my daughter says.
Yes, I agree, it's wyrd.

There are forty-eight trillion,
six hundred and ninety-five billion,
nine hundred and ninety-nine
thousand and sixty-two things
in my daughter's life.
And one of them has changed.

The potation has poured itself out.
It can not be put back into the bottle.

Cattail fluff floats by,
gossamer hooks
and bloated ovum.

He Is Fishing (Suite)

MUSIC

i. Early afternoon

My son pulls
a perch from the lake,
and then another.

Around us in the bushes
the blackberries husk, mature, ripen,
almost fall of their own volition.

Yet reluctant to pain,
my son passes, on his line,
each fish to me,

and I pass my hand
down and along their spiked spines,
palming their rapturous bodies—

a gentle kind of torture—
work the arc of the hook to release them

and then fling them back to the dark water.

While he practices patience
again and again,
I roam off in widening circles,

filling my hands
with the sweet stain of fall,
blackberry thorns plucking, with authority, at my legs.

Later I will pass these blackberries to him,
with hands that would have, a moment before,
pressed the shit core right out of a worm.

He'll eat, smile, then cast again.

The welts along my legs will ripen
from stain
to something more sinister.

    ii.   Late afternoon

As fire-red mushrooms
push through the forest's pine bed,
I run in the rain,

trying to keep below the black cloud
of my latest back injury
which had me unable to walk well yesterday.

The red mushrooms call to mind
the bellies of the perch
my son pulled from the lake this morning.

I begin to dream of him
fishing with his grandfather.
This is how he goes, I think, *finally, clutching his chest.*

Like this, I tell my son in my mind, *he went like this, to fish,
and to his favorite grandson
no better end imaginable.*

Across the trail in front of me
lies a newly fallen birch tree,
cut into by beaver teeth

at   five   almost   equal   intervals.

Like music, I think.

I stop and bend down
into my body's pain,
touch the perfect marks,

first with fingertips,
and then with lips.
Like this, I say aloud, to no one, but to everything.

It Was This Big

— in memoriam Mike Izor, age 57

at this point in witnessing the line to the mind snaps

The son in the shower with the father,
laving the crinks and crevasses of long legs, scrawny arms,
and sweeping soapy suds over unused muscle, emaciated bone tufts,
    the balls.

The father taught the son
how to tie flies,
how to thread the meager body mid-stream without falling,
how to delicately sweep the ambit of air with his line.

    one part of the person goes off after the animate
    one part is spirit soaring without aim by way of mind

He lived as though he were constantly primed to catch the big one,
sporting worn jeans and his litefelt fedora.
He strode, pretty much unfaltering, a ready knife on his thigh.

After the service there is suffering
and a cessation of suffering.

    again—*rupture*

A tall man, he would not acclimate to his urn.
Where is his hat, I wonder.
Where there are sandwiches, incongruities lie.

I wade off through an inkling of days in search of his knife.

An Untitled Rothko

It was as if what he'd reached once—call it a truth, meaning, or absolute—was so vitally important to him that he had to keep on trying to get to it again. A point in infinity where beauty, truth, feeling and experience come together; a level of reality which makes all other levels of reality seem pale, uninteresting, insignificant.
    — Geneviève Vidal on Rothko

i. The river, a band of steel-shine bent into an ingot of color that defies a name
ii. the banks, sheaves of wheat shaken in the forsaken's clenched fist
iii. the fish, flickerings, crescents plunging the lunky conveyor belt moving up the mainstream

The son's cuffs are folded three times as he wades with weighted
> pockets in pursuit of the threading,
a streak of light, an aberration of color, a hovering, a playful patient
> presence,
a puzzle piece never quite fitted or still.

He is fishing.

Seed

tōgarashi
omoikonasaji
mono no tane

the red pepper
I do not belittle
seedlings
—Bashō

I keep a chestnut
in the breast pocket of my secondhand leather jacket.
When I picked it I thought of (I don't know why) my mother.

The last time my first husband and I made love
I knew my womb, because of my mind, was tipped at such an angle
that no seed would germinate *there*.

This is also a true story.
Our children and I collected acorns to use for a project we had not yet imagined.
They exploded into weevil larvae all over the floor.

What's Good for You

*Always be true to these things.
They are all there is.*
— Kenneth Rexroth

It's true, I admit, I don't like man.
I mean, I love him because I have to,
kind of like how I know I need to eat my vegetables.
And when I do it's something in my body
that loves them for me.
It's true, in order to stay sane
I go away from man and what man has created.
As in: the architecture of days and nights.
I don't mean art. I mean commerce.
And sometimes art as commerce.
I mean, I need the trees and the rocks and
the terrible torment of the rugged world
to scourge me of my dirty human foibles.
It's true, we fuck up too often.
And it's also true, we bend our grace into staffs and snakes.
I mean, I've come across snakes in the wilderness
and I've loved them. Real snakes, that is.
I've stepped over them
in fear with reverence
—that quick strike of warning:
when it comes to survival
one never knows for sure what nature will do.
How unlike the snakes of mankind,
venomous, self-aware and cruel,
imagination fork-tongued for power.

But the other night as I was leaving the grocery store
and my children were lazily joking in the car

and we were about to go to McDonald's, it was twilight.
A father and his child (a boy or a girl, I couldn't tell),
were walking in the snow from a nearby Canadian Tire.
And as they walked, smeared shadows, they talked.
Not quite hearing all their words,
I got the sense it was something fantastical,
the little one saying something
and the father playing along, cajoling,
Oh, ya, me too, I feel the same.
The child was trying to outdo the dad,
something about the milky way, god, the universe.
But again the father accepted, provoked, *Ya, ya, me too.*
And they walked toward the grocery store.
And they were small against the coming-fast night.
And the smile I wore was a shield against the pain I felt
for I ripped in a sudden rush of kinship.

It's Late

The curtain between our rooms is open.
I have fallen asleep with my broken glasses on,

holding *Anna Karenina,* heavy in so many ways,
its pages rifled open but eased back into the blankets

like a sleeping infant, my own hands yet creased
as though around a bottle. My son has forgotten

why he's come in and so instead just says, Mum,
remember when your moccasins were too big

for my feet? Playfully he demonstrates he can't even
squish the width of his toes inside them. We both seem

amazed that this was the truth and now the truth has
changed. He leaves. The curtain falls. I take off my glasses.

Turn off the light. Remind myself to wrap
his birthday presents in the morning.

iv.) **kya-kya-kya**
wherein jackdaw experiences
distress and excitement

One Shade Away from Never Having Been

Sometimes it seems the world is too damn big,
too many variables, too many two-faced blessings.
Trying to be calm or at ease in the flux and pulse
of the interminable motion seems impossible.

So, after an hour or two of trying
to settle into the churning miasma,
slipping in and out (only to slip in and out again) of the turnstile
    of what's possible, of what might become possible,
    of what's imaginable and what's unimaginable (but imagine),
    of what's within control, what's uncountably (count) beyond
—you try to think a garden.

A garden, a reasonable plot of land,
a chosen section to churn, turn, mind,
mend, sow and nurture.
This, you think, only this
you will concern yourself with.

The tilling begins,
and quite quickly you discover
a nearby oak root has wended its way in your way
and belies an easy sifting.

    Work, grinding and assertion.

And then the soil, once turned, reveals it's denuded.

Or is a draw for cutworms, wireworms, or root maggots.

Or the tall tomato plants were planted
too tightly together with excitation,

wicking blight into your lives.

A groundhog burrows into the plot
through the depths of your unreasonable mind.

So you make yourself a smaller garden.

And then smaller again.

Until the garden is only a couple shakes of earth,
the size of a picnic basket.
In which you plant a single matronly tomato.
Sow a solitary seed to become a gentleman bean pole.
Blow a breathful of seedlets to make lettuce babies.

But this isn't the truth.
You know immediately the ruse.
And so you keep downsizing
until your hands are gone.
And there is only rock
with a scrim of soil.
A plant or a tree.
An unnamed weed.
And maybe a bird.
An insect.
Or wind.

Only the chance of the soil meeting seed.
Only the arbitrary and unlikely sowing of life.

Only then do you sleep.

Tangerine

...being no longer only.
— Jack Gilbert

There have been times
when all forests have been folded
and all their darkness
funneled by the folds
to flood the inkwell of my mind.

That was back when my heart,
old goat,
munched up leaves,
with no emotion.

Then one night
I happened upon the spiraled rind
of a tangerine
set loose
by someone else's fingers,
left to glow in the moonlight.

Residue of freshness.
Orange curves. Robust clues.

Lanterns began to light my path—
Who might have walked
while unbraiding Fibonacci's thumbprints?

Suddenly—angels were possible.

Sex with You is a Strange Violin

It is not to lower the pail
to steal a sloppy drop of water.
It's not geometry to want.
Not controls to fiddle.
Not to lift.
Not aerodynamics.
Not control tower.
Not diving beneath.
No subterfuge.
Not to cram air into the vial
nor to trace the outer cast.
Not braille.
Not sonic.
Certainly not ergonomic.

But to bend the violin,
to feel through the body its curved harrow.

Statistics, 2012

I cannot think of Galway Kinnell
without thinking of his little boy Fergus
and his pajamaed body tucked so pleasurably
between the pages of his parents' bodies.

So when my boy comes in, crying out in anguish,
I don't know if it is for the horror of crashing bodies,
the terror of fascinating desire,
or because the man on top of me is not his father.

Genealogy, Hope and a Christmas Turkey

...There is within me a persistent unrest, a yearning I cannot define, imperative and absorbing... I want to hope, I should like to know. I need limitless illusions....

— Senancour

The first time Christmas died for you
    you were ten or so,
but you didn't know it had died;
    you only knew that something in the air was different,
or worse,
    something inside of you,
as though a casket had become the casing of your body.
    So you bore down with your reserves and continued to learn
and demonstrate how necessary it was/is to lie to yourself
    to be able to lie convincingly to others.
You continued to open presents marked *from Santa,*
    opening your mouth
as you opened the gifts, wide,
    in a wild feigned frantic felicity (slightly demonic).

Then Christmas bloomed again a few years later
    in its deceit,
rose a little like an awkward
    off-white balloon,
and became something else—
    mild.
And you became comfortable enough
    echoing down your long pine throughways
knowing that all of the others,
    older than you,
must be sloughing somatically down their personal corridors too.
    And anyway, strange,

your mother still sang on Christmas mornings,
    arias, badly,
while she pulled the turkey, to baste, temporarily out of the oven,
    she an emblem of a genial kind of happiness which might be
    sustained.

Then you had kids and you hijacked their happiness.
    Oh, you were only too willing
to jump aboard that train of naiveté and delirious delight,
    wonder the highest of highs, and weren't you a junkie?
Were you completely daft?
    Did you not then realize that that train was the same as your
    own,
which, in time, would wind down?
    And did you not then realize that that pain, second time around,
would be more acute than ever?
    When Christmas died for your kids
the casket of your body become the coffin of your mind,
    future twilights (hope fires) stifled.

How remarkable your mother remained,
    her ragged perm highlighted by the wet jewels from the hot
    turkey,
her 6 a.m. to 4 p.m. rising and falling, faltering, recovered, warbling
    arias,
    her simple kitchen joy which maintained you through your most
    brutal crises in belief,
your inevitable discoveries and despondencies
    and your hard-earned, time-willing, recoveries from trauma.

A Winter's Night, A Love Poem

We're doing it again, opening the door, going out into the night
that bites, where we won't see a thing with the snow being picked
up and blown in frenzied wisps as though a woman is madly
sheering ribbon. The horses must be bedded, the hinges latched,
the chickens lured to become dumbly numb, as though tucked into
a quiet pocket. It will seem hollow inside the barn except
for the occasional boot laid down. One might think of an unplayed
organ, or a town hall before anyone scrapes a chair, or long after.
Once we found a cow frozen to the southbound fence as though
she had wandered off sensing better weather. One eye was stuck
to the snow like a grape dried to a wound, the other a perfect pond
frozen over. It seems strange on this exposed night, this night like
pages in a book blown open, that we should ever be brave enough.
I pull my scarf tight. Walk past you to the stubborn door. Push
with firm abdomen. Strong wind—even the night offering us
this one last chance to stay behind. But we advance together,
out into the inhospitable drum, where stars exist somewhere.

Anthem

Standing at the kitchen island bored and in just one tick of the clock
    regretting it,
your daughter asks if you liked school, and you look backwards,
something opening up there and you see as a surprise to yourself,
not that you liked it exactly, but that you didn't like being at home
    more—
it was always a little like "This Be the Verse" by Philip Larkin, but a
    little unlike it too,
as it must be for everyone, even your daughter standing beside you
in her black jeans, black toque (*beanie,* she corrects you) and army
    boots,
gobbling back black coffee because that's the thing to do, the thing to
    move you
from a. to b., and what is adolescence if not the elevated surge of
    momentum,
screaming hard, shaking the shot, yearning with an angst-bound face
    to be put into tomorrow,
and didn't you want to go hard, hard, away from your mother's house,
which was full of food, comfort-thick cushions and deafening blows
of bills, coffee, smokes and a whole bunch of quickly going nowhere,
the television propped open as a kind of sinkhole pulling on, but not
    in,
gathering everything together in a static halo of a twenty-year-long
    holding in of
stale breath, pork chops, car repairs and vegetables for dinner,
that would, sooner or later, all get flushed with no aplomb, down the
    shitter?

And now you, what do you do, *do?* What do you have to offer
your daughter, the complex scratch of vascularized cross-hatchings,
pen-knife scribed notches on the hood of the rolling stars of coffin?
You, you sit! On your couch and read poetry. Then walk *(enlightened)*

in forests,
feeling not so much elevated for not having the TV as a backdrop,
but rather that you've narrowly escaped the clutches of that thing,
that *thing* which lurked behind mediocrity's distracting drone in the eighties
and now looms, hashtag, selfie, tumbler, crotch-grab, beneath social media's hipster pillow,
only to (my god!) get excited about—what exactly? But, oh, how you are excited!
Turkeys trotting down snow-covered roads leaving their foot-bound scribbles,
foxes winding literally and metaphorically through vetch,
the way Amy Clampitt incurvates and veers through the haystack of words
to *outfinden* (c. 1300, Middle English: to discover by scrutiny),
the confident, yet plebeian exegesis, through, of all arousing things—*grass!*—
the inarguable answer (the only kind possible), homely and craftless, to existential existence.

She throws back her black coffee as splash, it barely touching her lips, rolls eyes, puffs bangs,
black hair (from a box), rolls shoulder to book bag and confidently, with grand yet casual chagrin,
kicks closed the door on you behind her, to go to school, which she hates, leaving you, ditto,
to find her way by way of vascular flow, *fucker!* to the vastly more higher still,
titillating finally (no longer blandly wrong), *right!* raucous, crashing, important life.

Three Teens Sleep in a Tent

> *...the waste of the seed of the self*
> *Stains in the shaggy hide, and they know it not.*
> — William Everson

At first I think of stray mittens,
the two red wagons staggered
through the long backyard,
cast-offs on the journey
toward the mouth of the tent,
the wood charred and plinked
upon itself, a child's
abandoned game of pick-up sticks,
but with the spring rain ripe
and the grass burning green,
I'm awoken sober as to clatter
to the world's eternal awakening.
The idea of their bodies glows,
ancient dark flames fanned
between rind and dense electric flesh,
innards of the Rouge Vif d'Etampes,
the yard looking less like childhood
and more like a gaping seduction,
wagons, singed wood,
half-burned sticks that pierced,
then taunted and flaunted
their marshmallow's skins,
socks and gutted slick packages,
all their taking off-s, dismantlings,
while they sleep inside, those wild
young buffalo, those purring heaps
of husky wilderness,
inside the tent,

inside themselves,
inside inside inside,
ten times the size their shells!
They have no understanding,
those terrible living beasts,
aroused through ambrosial selves,
drunkened by world and each;
can't tell their hooves
from hands or feet;
don't care.

A Rural Mom Warns Her Daughter about
Dangers in the City

There will be the whole blanket, of course.
There will be the basket, the bread.
There will be the lovers and the seagulls
and the children playing and laughing.
Look, one of them will have a yellow kite.
Look, one of them will have fallen onto her side
like a squat red triangle.
Not to worry—
there will be help to right it.
There will be one shape happily being swallowed
by another. A blue rectangle will eat clouds.
New black circles will take in pieces of pie
which first took in apples.
And the waves will come to a stop there at the shore.
One can trust certain horizons,
as the park will start and stop inside the city.
But remember, in the park, on the blanket,
there will be a grouse's heart, beating there, beneath the napkin.
There will be that knife, leftover, after cutting bread.

The Roan

Suddenly he raises his proud face,
snorts gasconades of filth and fire,
concusses the ground
stamping his place.

Like gneiss: *I too have raced plains!*
Laboriously plucked my way over mountain ranges
and braced through the depths of the sea's rage!
I, too, dare love.

He rolls his mad eyes and exhales
the green decay of his fanatical single-mindedness.
My son, fifteen, meets me this time at the city's gate,
a comparable specimen, perhaps more.

Birdsong

I pull the blanket
from his shoulder
and off his broad feet
and touch the
nearly-forbidden skin,
newly exposed,
as I have been doing
every morning
since his birth.

Outside a bird empties
a little of its sugar
out of a sac
from the branches
of our basswood.

Do you hear it, I ask him,
as he nudges away from me,
nosing back into his sheets,
closing once again in on the zero
of his personal sleep.

Yes, he nods.

Well, I say,
as you drive into the city,
don't forget it.

The Mother

The last bladder is emptied,
the last gleek shot into the sink,
the last struggling out of and into,
the last—somewhat grooming,
the last sandwich flogged to its plastic compartment,
the last backpack retrieved from the floor,
the last gangly stumbling,
the last repeated good day utterance, love you, etc.,
the last kicking of the front door.

The mother is alone.
The house stands still for a moment
in its terrible shock of silence.
Then shakes off its cold blanket.
The mother leans into herself like tilted kindling,
a neanderthal, or philosopher returned to her cave.
She begins to make the fire.
It doesn't matter what she makes the fire with.
The mother burns.

v.)
wherein Jackdaw can be trained
to imitate human speech

Children of the Imperceptible

Jungle parasite, rare ugly ass-flower, each bloom battles the clock,
many dead (most) before buds even open, and those that do—mere days.
You, *Rafflesia,* itching to thrive, but dying in the meat-rot heat heaven of
    Indonesia.

The mind is three heavens deep and two hells wide
and night in Antarctica is nine long fathoms unfathomable,
nothing but the length of the penguin's regal body
consuming the height of the regal body to quantify it.

Deliberate priest of the cold, father of eighty-one percent soon dead, frozen
    stiff, utvak,
unsentimental chunk of ice and flesh, you, sacrosanct, yet with no
    measure of sorrow, history, self.

I am trying to understand.

We ask—why something instead of nothing,
when only one one-billionth of the something has mind enough to ask it.

I am trying to understand.

Does love live in the cells?
Does it leach, propagate, thrive, survive?
Do angels have hemoglobin?

I am trying to understand.

Even though the gamut between Indonesia and Antarctica is wondrous,
is it enough?

Body of Complaint

Heavy and swollen with sweat,
bending and straining to lift boxes,
a steady litany of complaints to hone my place:
damned job, work so hard, so little pay,
hungry indifferent kids, no thanks.
It's not a wonder I don't...
It's not a wonder I...

But what might I *do* or say
beyond this test of—what?—endurance?—
this sickly lot of little to earn my space,
which isn't so bad, really, I imagine,
but can't actually will myself to say
in my deeper soul except upon
convenient and leisurely occasions.

Last night sunk in a self-funk on the couch,
a bowl of munchies on my chest,
fat food to stuff in my fat face,
a nature show clicked on for my indulgence—
the emperor penguins in Antarctica with their eggs...
the emperor penguins in Antarctica...
the emperor penguins...

Mare

When is it we come to the realization
 that all things are wandering away?
  — Charles Wright

I.

I am driving by, watching.
Things like this always happen
inside the momentum of other things.
Time is like a waterfall,
someone says.

II.

In the center of a green pasture
four corpulent mares have gathered
in a circle to confer.
What they are discussing
is the listless colt
lying like a sable fur
upon the dew-lit grass.
One mare, probably the mother,
is stomping her hoof,
tearing up divots of soil.
Certainly, she thinks,
if I translate this angst
through this body—!

The four of them stare,
one unblinking eye
staring into the green eye of earth
which doesn't blink either.

This is how my grief for you works.
This is how it changes nothing.

Real Things; Not Junk—
    Swimming in the Aux Sables River

> *I am drawn to that state of emptiness which I can never get to, in which you are open to real things and not the junk of this world.*
> — Charles Wright

Lowering myself
beneath the lucid screen of water
to discover the two dimensions are three.

Pale smooth skin in water.
A body deserves to feel this good.
That's all.

Treading the blackness
is like brushing against van Gogh's
eddies in *The Starry Night*.

Further out there is a dangerous one,
undertow,
lurking beneath the mantle.

I'm between there
and the sharp rock I must climb to get out
with the serrated circumference.

Far beyond the pines of this poem
Christians and Muslims and Jews, or so-calleds,
are fighting and/or killing or being killed.

Overhead a vulture circles
narrower and nearer.

A body *deserves* to feel this good.

Helpless. And actualized. As the embryo is about to pass through the mother's wrap into the three dimensions of life.

The Shine on the Road's Blacktop When It Rains

It's 2016. South, Trump's just been elected.
Here, thank God, after Harper (no angel)
a fairly new Liberal government.
Everywhere, hotter than average temperatures.
It's early evening but black as night, November.
My teenage daughter and I are on the couch
watching, together, Nina Simone
deliver her 1976 performance of "I Wish I Knew
How It Would Feel to Be Free." A master craft,
how she mocks the historical white audience
tinkling *you-fool* lightly
all over the classics encoded in the piano,
plucking the irony back
and then wringing its neck
skillfully
in her evening gown,
her black forehead glistening,
after all, a girl is gonna goddamned eat,
even the bird,
even the sacred one she finally sets flying.

    No parent can say anything and know that she is heard.

Ms. Simone's evening gown is shining.

    No parent can explain just where we've been.

    Watch her body, I want to say. See how she
    thrashes in pure measure and wry splendor.
    When she moves, even a little,
    she is moving against some*thing*.

But it's me my daughter's watching out of the corner of her eye.
Me. And I cry against the wings. I cry with longing
and with shame.

Cancer (Suite)

Healthcare

I'm in an MRI machine
and I don't want to be
in an MRI machine, and
so with my eyes closed
I visualize the swamp
I was in front of yesterday.
There's a swathe of fresh
air in front of my face, a
whole orbit of it
shaped like a pulpit.
And whatever this MRI
is looking for,
I don't want it to find it.
Gonna hide it behind Jupiter.
(There, just did.)
Gonna do just what I want to,
get up out of this predicament,
the one that keeps blasting
ridiculous ray gun noises
in my ears, and I'm gonna walk
clear over to where that
woodpecker is pounding.
It's a pileated,
and by god, he's gorgeous.
And even though my feet
don't move, here I am
looking up at this creature
that god must have taken
extra care with to get so
perfect. Are you kidding me,
pound a tree twenty times

a second with a force
a thousand times that of gravity!
And that red! How is it that a
color can wring an organ?
Anyway, while I'm at it,
if this is all possible (and
it is 'cause here I am in an
MRI not having a panic attack
and simultaneously hiking
my favorite swamp), I'm
going to visualize some
stable ice for those
starving polar bears;
gonna heap all the
neonicotinoids
into rolling papers,
just like the old timers
used to do with tobacco
(but now know better;
that stuff will kill you!),
and then shake it clear off
the face of the earth.
I'm going to do what seems impossible,
imagine a future for our kids.

RADIANCE

5. Begin at the End

Let's begin from the end, shall we? From where the long black cord with the camera, shoved up my ass, is inserted—but let's say *withdrawn*. Let's be gentle here. That's the point, isn't it, to take the pain of it and maunder it down to a low boil. To touch life where it's bearable and beautiful. So yes, we'll have to get farther back than here. Let's release the camera from its poor pilgrimage and put it back into the surgeon's hands.

4. The Procedure—Introduced

Let's have her laughing. The doctor's laughing at the joke I delivered just before the black swallowed my frontal lobe, as the snake conceals the egg in its belly. It's Valentine's day. A funny day for such a task. I mean, come on, to be buggered with a machine by a stranger.... I've asked her for my box of chocolates. What? None? Then she says, *This will be....* Then black.

3. The Inner Waiting Room

But what it is is that I am walking back into the waiting room. The second waiting room. The last. These things happen in stages. The white walls. Metal chairs. Everyone in sky blue, mint green. (Dignity or indignity—slippers?) We are staring. Staring at the walls as though they're screens. Although blank. Our lives must be playing on them. We're so attached. No one dares to move. Someone coughs. The cottons are so soft. You see, the world is good to us. It is remarkable how comfortable we are almost naked. Side-by-side strangers. A mercy of the body. I nearly kiss my arms. I'm such a loving skin. A man returns between the surgical doors from his future. Sits. Anxious. Waiting. A toilet flushes. Many of us have the simultaneous thought: *This is a very good idea.* I go to the bathroom to empty myself, or rather—fill with fluids.

2. The Restroom

I am standing after the void and dizzy. The mirror is a tricky thing to negotiate. This is the person who is at question? Me? Her? I nearly spit in disbelief. I can't join my image to my mind's thoughts. Some sewing has come undone. I struggle to make sense of the robe's ties, produce some knots. I look again, or—return to my initial visage. I hold the banister. Wipe. Tinkle. Yes, the yellow juice returns to me. This body will make this! This body is an act of art! My knees are bent. A small organ works inside. And clearly, so clearly, a thought opens up like a tent of knowledge over my shoulders, *Well, I'll be damned! Here I am before this procedure, before this new uncertainty.* Quite clearly a penumbra forms by the awning of my brow. I speak to the awning. *I didn't ask to be here.* I hear the words, *I did not ask my mother to bear me.* Is this hilarious or tragic? Or neither? As simple as the curve of this procedure, the timeline, the arc, the sweep, the impaling.

1. The Outer Waiting Room—Triage

We are in the first waiting room now. Someone calls my name. I am about to pour my feet back into the comfort of my socks. I am about to place each breast back into the bra's cradle. I am about to drive home. Pick up my phone. Five years cancer-free—order roses for my mom. Roses. I don't even know if they're appropriate. But their petals are so soft. Soft like the cottons we'll wear. But for now I am waiting with the others, each of us dying in different amplitudes, along different vectors, with different concussions, but all with the same conclusion. We are each in our chairs beside a wall of windows. Light is coming in in even sheets. A good room in which to take a photograph.

But light is springing out from each of us too. Out from our cunts. Our ass holes. Out from our eyes and mouths. We are warm in the cold hospital waiting room. Each of our meat-machines, here to be inspected, are levitating upon personal beams. Each of us unasked for. Present.

To Live

It's ten p.m. I'm eating cereal from a box thinking
about how innocent we all were four years ago.
It was winter then. Now it's fall. There was snow
everywhere and would be for months. I was waiting
on cancer results. I would live or die. While we waited
my husband and I would sit on the couch. The lights
of *Ikiru* would dapple our pale faces. I kind of loved
the ominous irony of it. (He gave it to me for Christmas,
not quite thinking it through.) I lived and now we're
here, the cereal a small concession to healthy eating.

I wait for an interruption on this white screen
to tell me you're also still alive.

Human Chain

I'm on my knees
at the river
funneling handful
after handful
of rich black dirt
into buckets.

A man wanders by.

Mutually interested,
we engage
in a brief discussion.

Introductory at first.

Then gaining in fervor.

Capped
    by an epiphany
like a fish being shot with a silver bullet fired straight from a
    thought
swimming in the mind.

Then I'm on my knees again.

Alone again.

Then with my daughter,
funneling handful
after handful
of rich black dirt
into buckets.

Eighteen years pass.

When she learns
I will die some day,
she rises,
taking all but one
bucket.

Homecoming

Lack of use
hangs the old jean shirt
from the rusty peg
in the freezer room
over the freezer
(whose sealed edge has enervated
and therefore harbors
a moldy corruption)
just opposite the torn screen
on the door out
to the natural world.

We're moving
when my son's eye
(by case of reduction of stuff)
rests for a moment again
on the soft blue hue
and his hand chooses
to pluck,
then sweep
up and around
the old puckering of the neck
which is quickly,
its proximity advancing,
becoming familiar.

But something stops him, it,
mid-air, mid-drift,
from returning
to his body
after four abandoned years,
some visual cue

like seeing/sensing
a sudden caliginous body
threatening
from the woods' edge.

Bees have taken over the creases
of the assailable arm pits,
have loaded the shirt
with a mash of nacreous bluster
that shines and fluctuates
between *piceous* and *glister,*
like space and god and the incomprehensible idea of *forever*.

Gentrification

I'm sitting in my car in the old downtown,
watching a man who wears a red toque,
in my rear view mirror,
conceal something in his jacket.
He dashes across the tracks
just as a train approaches. A shopkeep
opens a door and looks to where the man was.
The train rumbles through the neighborhood.
Abruptly the door is closed.
Across the road *Roy Roy Roy*
is painted over
every second-floor shuttered window
of the bankrupt brick furniture store,
creating a kind of bland art
pleasing in its sparseness and symmetry,
if you stare hard enough.
"Modern," if it were the 1960s.
There are three ground floor windows.
In one, a fire extinguisher.
Another must have a leak as it,
despite the cold, is varnished, sweaty.
We simply sell for less, in yellow paint
on orange, is broken up in part by two fans
that turn only when the air catches them.
Vegetarian fare and fair trade coffee shops,
a stripper's club and the auxiliary
poorly heated apartments, ebb out from
Roy Roy Roy's.
My son has just auditioned for art school.
He has been accepted.
A green shopping cart lies on its side
just off the sidewalk.

A real estate sign curls in the third ground floor
window touting 20 000+ square feet
of forsaken capitalist kingdom.
Who might they keep out of art school and why?

Jacquard

It displeases me that he smokes,
so he smokes only mugwort.

He is working an O'Keeffe print
from an old *Life* magazine.

The flower now smells of ash.

What he cuts bears a cauterization
of his, and his alone, hands.

He frames the flower, *Black Iris, 1926*,
and a little bit of the accompanying text.

Hangs it.

Then we carry in the couch.

There are two sides to the cushions.

He could place them beige side-up
but instinctively prefers the sprawling floral print.

We sit beside one another and consider
O'Keeffe's work:

>it's a fire wearing an iron chastity belt,

>a snapshot of coral reef with undulating seaweed,

>how my labia still carry the christening
>of his cranium.

"Nobody sees a flower—really—
it is too small—we haven't time...."

He lights one of his shabby
hand-rolled cigarettes. Inhales.

Burning inherits the edges.

Nature and Nurture

Your daughter
(who will never have children,
and while she was a child
hated being yours)
will forget Mother's Day.

But, the day before
she will come to you
with her sweating terrarium,
a bounteous bowl of earth,
moss and weather,
cupped beneath her full breasts,
and ask you the name of that plant
she sees sometimes on walks
in the woods (where you
often walk as well)
with its wee crinkled digits
a particular shade of green-blue,
that produces little red caps.
Somewhat like this,
she'll say, pressing her face
to the bits of green life
that spread lacy fingertips
to press against glass—
and before she is done asking you,
you will already be answering
about the symbiotic relationship
that is the strange life of *British soldiers.*

Decibel

I'm quiet at the back of the group of girls, nervous.
There are perfectly packaged presents on the table.
It's not my birthday and the gift I am giving is
mediocre. I'm in grade five. We're talking about
our families again. If I hold my toes just right,
despite the holes, they all stay inside the casing.
I don't want to say anything. If I do, I lose concentration.
Now I'm getting out of his silver car. It's called *the pickle*.
I never know why it's called *the pickle* and I don't
care. I'm slamming the door. Apparently vaginas
are not enough. Unless they are quiet. I do not
have a quiet vagina. I'm really pissed off. So what
if I've taken only one film class. I know shit. I say it.
There's another vehicle. We're going fast. Again.
This becomes a habit. He actually tells me to shut
the fuck up and—*put your head out the window.*
I actually go on to marry this man. Ah, he's not all
bad. Actually, I am. Or, sometimes my moral code
can be called into question. I'm on my knees in bed.
I've been laughing all evening. My sides are sore
and my vision kind of blurry. Back when I dated
the guy with *the pickle,* I had a roommate. We
laughed a lot. She and I had this joke that we were
IT. I was the *I* and she was the *T.* Now, just like then,
I write a few poems. She's accomplished, a lawyer.
Tonight I've been laughing with my daughter.
Laughing and laughing and fucking laughing.

Regarding the Fullness of Emptiness and Silence

It was some time in my forties that I turned
from being the drunk man in a football jersey at the party
into a bison, and with my last thrust of hairy hormones
ran full force all over my stinking penned-up field.
When I grew tired I knew the candles had been blown out.
Then I morphed down low into the furtive fox
that had been waiting to become my body.
Now I sit lightly, as still as a feather
caught slightly in the sedge at the edge of the field,
watching, abiding.

vi.)
wherein Jackdaw reconciles
with the world

Centripetal Force and a Lull in the Stratosphere

I looked up and found myself inside of it.

    But how astonishing.

I would never have known which door to take to enter it.

It was halfway over before I realized, my eyes big on my hands,
on my own two hands,
my senses swollen as though by bees,
my mind convinced of abnormalities come alive as though I'd been
    slipped LSD.

It lasted long enough for me to peruse the convenience store shelves
for canned potatoes and mushrooms, locate them, dusty, in strange
    places
(separate aisles), the potatoes next to the ludicrous event of canned
    beets.

    Canned beets! For crying out loud, who could have imagined!

I could smell the old floor. The walls drew nearer.
This was my convenience store. This was my life.

    Somehow I had caught up with it!

I stood inside of it with a delighted nervous vertigo, oddly at home.

Even later still, at home at the stove-top, the venison sausage
    sputtering,
spitting its juices, the cans canted, the vegetables singeing to a crisp
convincing and true, I drank a beer, a cold one, and I'll be damned if
my feet weren't bare on the kitchen floor in full contact.

    My hand handled the spatula!

I was planted through a thread in my head by the rank aroma
and cleansed with the cloth that passed by me as a breeze
carrying the kitchen window's simulacrum of garden growing waist-
    deep cilantro.

    Everything was right.

I had impostured myself for forty-odd years and finally,
for a moment, found myself directly inside of my life.

It Seeks Cracks and Enters

The cats were busy in the basement
rolling their nature through their paws,
playing the life right out
of the little mice that sought
fall refuge inside, returning them
to their embryonic hyphens.

While in the center of the floor,
an autumn bee clutched and clawed
its way toward the sump pump dirt,
like a man in a desert toward an oasis.

I scattered and praised the cats,
their eyes confused by the dull little deaths,
and laid the shroud of a sock
over the bumblebee,
wanting to spare them a sting
upon their curious faces.

This bee would not rise in spring.

And yet the veil I carried it in
startled me with the intensity of its agitation.
Maybe the bee had only hours left to live,
yet as I climbed the stairs and opened
the outside door, I felt its whole being buzz,
a marbled metal fabric vibrating with insistence.

Rarity Keeps the Raven at Bay

I walked down by the river today
where we were so young
in our forties, new together,
that place where one spring
you tipped me against a tree
and drank the sweet sap of blossoms,
the rest of the trails beating their
green wings keeping observers
at bay, or beckoning the brave ones
to hide behind the birches and turn
their eyes to diamonds
with the force of our scene.

Can you believe it, that winter
we walked up the river, not
caring to know any better,
tempting the ice to break?

As I walked down today
where the trillium sing in hordes
each springtime, a vitality
flared my veins and light
drew tunnels from my eyes
like rock salt. Small black plants,
like miniature curled dock
(I will have to learn their name),
dared one full monosyllabic testament
against the winter whiteness.
Equipped with these old
easier times I could hear
and see more clearly,
like before we began to learn

again, in our second lifetime,
the daily nomenclature of deaths

dispensed like blades.

Meditation Beside an Unkempt Lot

Say and savor this:

Betula alleghaniensis,
Juglans nigra,
Populus balsamifera,
Populus tremuloides,
Acer saccharinum,
Quercus velutina,
and *Prunus pensylvanica* or—pin cherry,
all movement above a low-lying bedding of bracken,
a list of plants and trees I experience—sway and caesura,
but don't know the names of except for the duration of this poem.

It is early Sunday morning and the breeze has not taken on any heat.

The leaves, with their various shapes and textures,
are passing with the wind, one way and then the other,
showing their topsides, then bottoms,

their two faces required for the being of their one body.

I am walking with wet hair but am warmed, and my hair is drying.
Tossed and tousled about my face, my vision isn't less,

but because of this sentient involvement, has evolved to become more.
The name that I sometimes go by is not needed. *Isn't.*

Grappling with Gratitude

Grapple (grăp'l) *verb,* to be human.

One of these times will be real.

Well, they all are.

But we grapple with definitions.

One of these times will be *final.*

The way my mother dies.

The body is a decisive point:

sleek for the extended *once.*

What freshness!—

Until the pendulum's dunk.

When I was little she sang and danced while making bread.

I was inspired to move too.

Thanks for the bread, Mum. I'm grateful.

Were her eyes closed when my father rocked this yeast into her?

Being friends was never the question. Just a nice adjunct.

She lies still while the black space of Neptune sews its net.

Except for the moaning as motion.

Except for the grappling with gratitude.

Atlas of Anatomy for an Artist

8:14 a.m. Another morning moving
down Highway 17, a superfluous pin
in a machine, one of those grass is grass
mornings, sunshine not suggesting ascension,
just evergreen, evergreen, evergreen.

But then three flames in my arms
and a sudden brick as my shoe,
a rotating of my weight as though
while riding a wave, recklessly
I feel cause to pull back on it.
My reaction though, how minuscule.
Design is declared
by the buck's move
                        ment,
remarkably calibrated.

Rack down.
Quarter turn of front hooves.
Unguligrade ready.

                    Accordion of body airborne.

Hind feet locked, loaded, concrete supplanted.

                    Released—
                          an enlightened flexing of the
    spine.

Unguligrade unguligrade simultaneous—

                          sail.

A bullet fired from a stationary rifle moves at the velocity imparted by the shell. A bullet fired from a speeding jet moves at the velocity imparted by the shell plus the velocity of the airplane. Similarly, the end of the femur moves at the velocity given it by the thigh muscles. The end of the tibia moves at the velocity given it by its muscles, plus the velocity of the end of the femur. One way of increasing speed is by adding parts, each moving at its own velocity. The overall velocity is then determined by the sum of the velocities of the parts.

The buck inside the breadth of a moment
an algebraic equation, an activated elegance.

I'm pulling back on my wheel like a drunk sailor.
We look into one another.

Pivot. Work. Pivot.

We do not collide.

Sometimes, when I see it,
I maneuver from sadness like this.
Sometimes I allow my soul its woe
and headlong, run toward it.

(Phil Myers, "Legs, Feet and Cursorial Locomotion")

Rust

The way time works the hinges of a house,
the way earwigs find their way into the kitchen,
the way hearing weakens, elbows pucker and cowboy boots
    crease,
the way nostalgia falls like dust all over tables,
the way the lilies blaze for just a moment,
—fire takes the curtains.

Citrus and Sugar

I arrived at the moment believing
everything happens eventually in arcs,
as in how stories are broadcast.
For instance, the gloss of marmalade slips off
the darkened mass of hacked kumquat,
to get distributed at the tip of the heel
of the lemon, lime and orange's peel.

And so as he held me I escaped his grasp,
encouraged up and outwards by the press of his arms,
and what fled from me was the sound of grief so sharp,
an articulated swerved curve, I could see and feel its arc
over me, a colorless rainbow with the lowering glow
of the reaper's scythe wielded, which goes:

grip, snaith, ring, tang, heel, beard, chine, toe, away from.

Culmination and Collapse

Okay—I'll say it again,
I'm okay with dying.
But this afternoon
with the smell of love-making
yet sweetening the room,
and you having just read aloud
your translation of Rilke's poem
"La Fontaine" (don't we learn
more and more from Rilke?),
the agglomeration of each sugared jewel
of each shared springtime
shining fuller and brighter,
accruing between us,
how might one not regret
that chickweed does not
surge past its confines of cornflower blue
to accomplish more than itself?
How might one accept that the pea,
planted each spring,
does not, year after year,
become greener
and greener?

Almost

    I.

Just past middle age,
is there a name for that,
a time to denote just after the crisis?

No, no word for that.

However,
the broad-stroked
musculature of the woodpecker
comes to mind,

or rather its lunatic red crest, watery stroke
and then its

just after—

    II.

Remember when you were younger and you were the key?

Remember feeling a thin pastel cylinder of dawn
over a lake
spinning like a wedding ring?

Remember the loon's cry?
Remember longing for it?

Remember being surprised when you yourself uttered it?

But also—not totally surprised.

III.

Speaking of art
(we were just reminiscing about the Chicago Art Institute
and how you were so sleep-deprived it was hard to make sense
    of anything,
but Whistler's muted *Nocturne: Blue and Gold—*
    Southampton Water,
still washes up at our feet),
when you look down,
Misery Bay in May,
not yet warm, everything wan:
beach sand, alvars, water,
everything's color draining:
a careful show of a well-worked elbow of driftwood,
the wretched stippling of creeping juniper,
bleached nearly bone-white crayfish legs
unattached to one another
but raised upon the glacial beach
as though praising.

In one ear, total absolution of waves.
In the other, a piquing of cedar trees at first blush empty,
but because of the clandestine clay-colored sparrows—
singing.

IV.

You're almost fifty.
If we're being honest, more than half-done,
and if nothing else, we try to be honest.

Here, upon your horizon, your pale halo of sky again,

the thinnest rim,

and then Georgian Bay
with its only slightly more brooding tincture,

another fringe,

and then grykes and dolostone pavements.

Infinity is out there, Erin.

You grab your collar closed around you.
You're cold.

Nearer, inside your scarf's loop,
infinity's in here, too.

And inside infinity?

You are married to it. Whatever it is.
You are married to it.
And you must make it speak.

vii.)

Agrarian Landscape with Fan Brush

Walking along between
the parceled farm fields,
the windows of heaven
keep passing over me,
squares of light
with painted casings
and finishing nails.
The wind sounds far off,
always arriving.
And is far off,
unless it is near.

Another winter has passed,
and I haven't learned to speak
another language
or paint as I had planned to.
No matter.
Even on this bland day
with its brittle wind,
the spruce that line one drive
are bristling light
amongst the birches
(no matter how dull
their glow,
it's breathtaking)
and keeping it.

One crow makes off
over a frozen field
of rawboned snow crust;
the other waits and plays
roadside, in the March mud.

I am thinking of Mahler's
Ich bin der Welt abhanden gekommen.
I wonder how much was accident
that I wasn't born a crow.
Or that I was born at all.

Wind cups the hemisphere,
howls.
Wind racks and tugs my hair.

Acknowledgments

    Previously published in...

Adirondack Review: "First Fort"
The American Journal of Poetry: "Statistics, 2012"
Dying Dahlia Review: "Sex with You Is a Strange Violin"
Equinox, Poetry and Prose: "One Shade Away from Never Having Been"
Gyroscope Review: "Agrarian Landscape with Fan Brush"
The Hamilton Stone Review: "Meditation Beside an Unkempt Lot"
Heartwood Literary Magazine: "Fingernails of Grain, Which Kept Safe my Childhood"
isacoustic: "Five," "An Untitled Rothko," "Jacquard"
Kestrel, A Journal of Literature and Art: "Atlas of an Anatomy for an Artist"
The Meadow: "Tangerine"
Natural Bridge: "A Rural Mom Warns Her Daughter about Dangers in the City"
On The Seawall: "Gentrification"
Open: Journal of Arts and Letters: "Centripetal Force and a Lull in the Stratosphere," "It Seeks Cracks and Enters," "Rarity Keeps the Raven at Bay"
Peacock Journal: "Hands Remember Best"
Poethead: "Considering Their Pale Faces," "Seed," "The Mother"
Poetry Ireland Review: "Tracks Disappearing over a Field"
Poppy Road Review: "Cantilevered"
Radius: "The Shine on the Road's Blacktop When It Rains"
Rust and Moth: "Pulling Carrots, Cabbage, Turnips, Late Fall"
Rat's Ass Review: "Jackdaw Chyak-Chyak," "Three Teens Sleep in a Tent"
San Pedro River Review: "A Winter's Night: A Love Poem"

Split Rock Review, Waters Deep: A Great Lakes Poetry Anthology: "Taking the Big Canoe to Childhood"
The Sunlight Press: "A Small Room with a Generous View"
Under a Warm Green Linden: "Almost"
The Windhover: "Because of Light"

Quotes

Constantine P. Cavafy, from "Hidden Things," *Collected Poems.* Princeton, NJ: Princeton University Press, 2009

William Everson, from "The Screed of the Flesh," *The Veritable Years.* Santa Rosa: Black Sparrow Press, 1998

Jack Gilbert, from "The Four Perfectly Tangerines," *Collected Poems.* New York: Alfred A. Knopf, 2014

Arvo Pärt, from *And Then Came the Evening and the Morning* documentary, via https://vimeo.com/79576837

Etienne-Jean-Baptiste-Pierre-Ignace Pivert de Senancour, from *Obermann.* 1804.

Kenneth Rexroth, from "A Sword in a Cloud of Light," *A Sword in a Cloud of Light.* 1979

Geneviève Vidal on Rothko, via http://vidal.genevieve.pagesperso-orange.fr/rothko/

Charles Wright, from "Waterfalls," *Caribou.* New York: Farrar, Straus, and Giroux, 2014

Charles Wright, from "A Conversation with Charles Wright," by Lisa Russ Spaar. *Image Journal* #102

www.ingramcontent.com/pod-product-compliance
Lightning Source LLC
Chambersburg PA
CBHW030336100526
44592CB00010B/710